PIANO · VOCAL · GUITAR

LADY ANTEBELLUM
NEED YOU NOW

Produced by
Alfred Music Publishing Co., Inc.
P.O. Box 10003
Van Nuys, CA 91410-0003
alfred.com

Printed in USA.

ISBN-10: 0-7390-6942-X
ISBN-13: 978-0-7390-6942-4

Management: Borman Entertainment, Santa Monica CA & Nashville TN
Booking: Creative Artists Agency, Nashville TN

Album Photography: Miranda Penn Turin
© 2010 Capitol Records Nashville

Album Art Direction: Joanna Carter & Jeri Heiden
Album Design: Ryan Corey, SMOG Design, Inc.
Album Production: Michelle Hall

 Alfred Cares. Contents printed on 100% recycled paper,
except pages 1–4 which are printed on 60% recycled paper.

CONTENTS

NEED YOU NOW

Words and Music by
DAVE HAYWOOD, CHARLES KELLEY,
HILLARY SCOTT and JOSH KEAR

*Alternate between open G and A on the 3rd string.

Need You Now - 7 - 1
34914

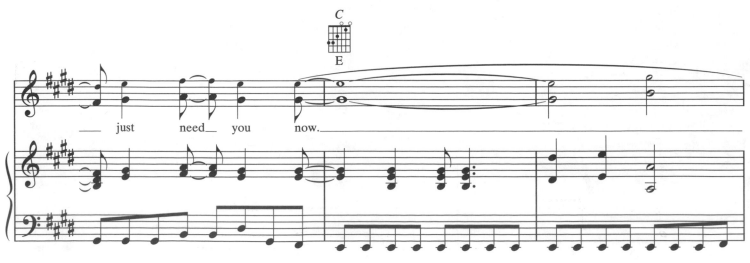

Female:

Oh,__ ba - by, I need__ you now.__

OUR KIND OF LOVE

Words and Music by
DAVE HAYWOOD, CHARLES KELLEY,
HILLARY SCOTT and MIKE BUSBEE

la - zy Sun - day af - ter - noon.

Female: I love the way that you are

liv - ing in the mo - ment, babe.

F: You get me laugh - ing with those

up for an - y - thing,

fun - ny fac - es.

nev - er wor - ried 'bout what

You some - how al - ways know just

peo - ple say.___ That's right.___ Oh,___ that's right.___ **M:** What we got___ is... **Both:**

what to say.___ That's right.___ Oh,___ that's right.___ **M:** What we got___ is... **Both:**

(Inst. solo ad lib....

That's our kind of love._____

Bridge:

...*end solo)* Oh, that's right, ba- by, you and I, what we got.__

Oh,___ that's our kind of love.___

One!   Two!   Three! Woo!
(Spoken:) Here we go!

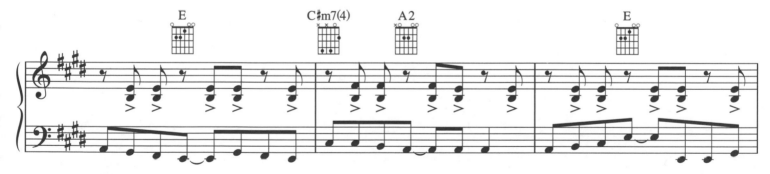

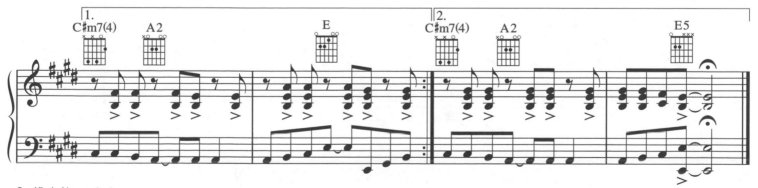

AMERICAN HONEY

Words and Music by
CARY BARLOWE, SHANE STEVENS
and HILLARY LINDSEY

Gtr. tuned:
⑥ = D   ③ = G
⑤ = A   ② = A
④ = D   ① = D

Moderately slow country rock ♩ = 84

Verse 1:

1. She grew__ up_____ on the side of the road_____ where the church bells__ ring_____ and strong__ love

*Original recording in D flat, guitar tuned down 1/2 step.

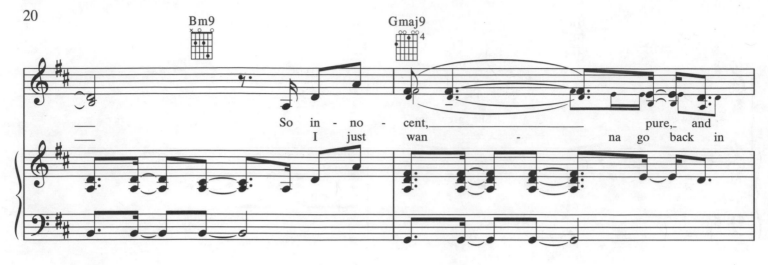

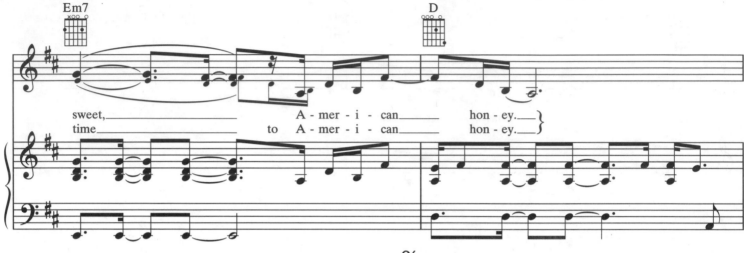

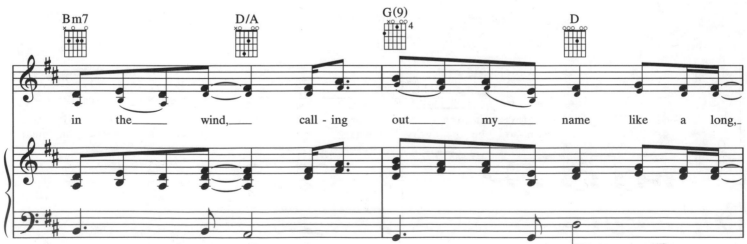

lost friend. Oh, I miss those days as the

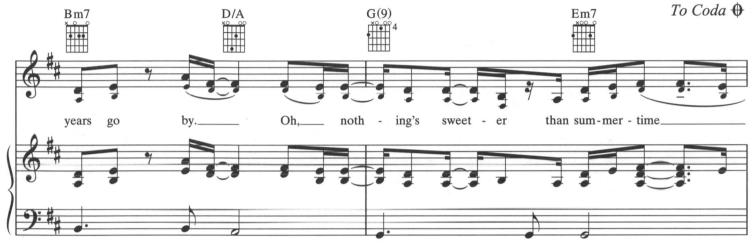

To Coda

years go by. Oh, noth-ing's sweet-er than sum-mer-time

1.

and A-mer-i-can hon-ey.

3. Get caught in the and A-mer-i-can

2.

hon - ey._____ I've gone for

Bridge:

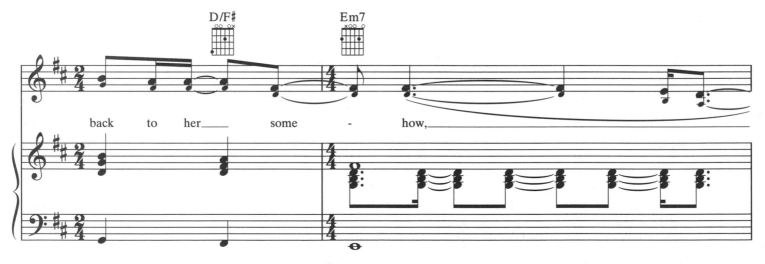

so long, now._____ I got - ta get

back to her____ some - how,_____

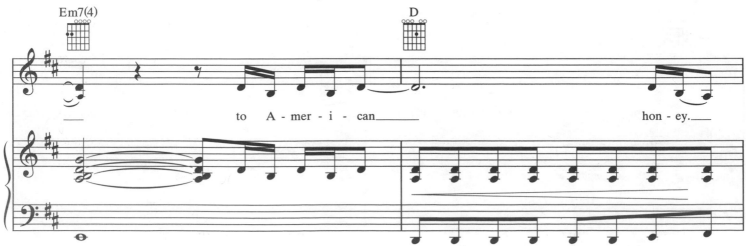

____ to A - mer - i - can_____ hon - ey.____

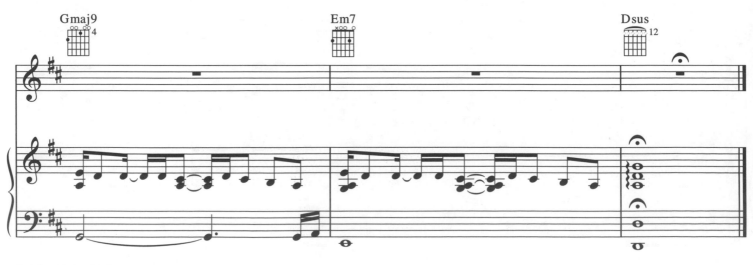

HELLO WORLD

Words and Music by
TOM DOUGLAS, TONY LANE
and DAVID LEE

Verse 1:

1. Traf - fic crawls,___ cell___ phone calls,___ talk ra - di - o screams_

Hello World - 12 - 1
34914

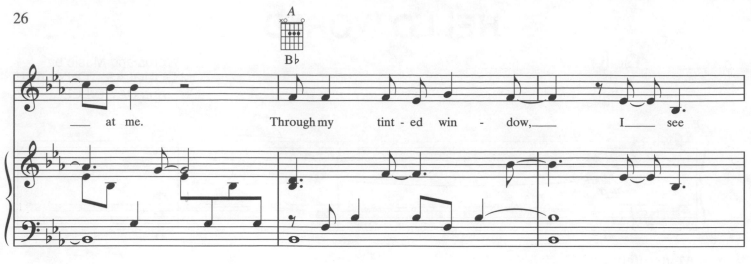

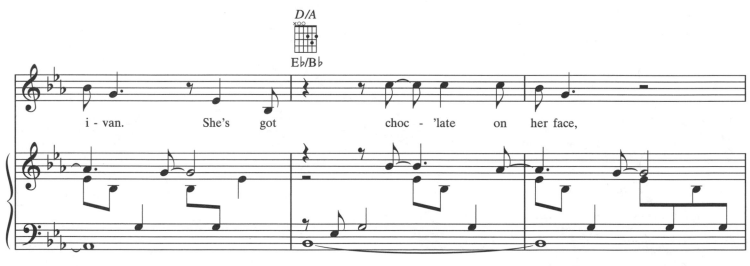

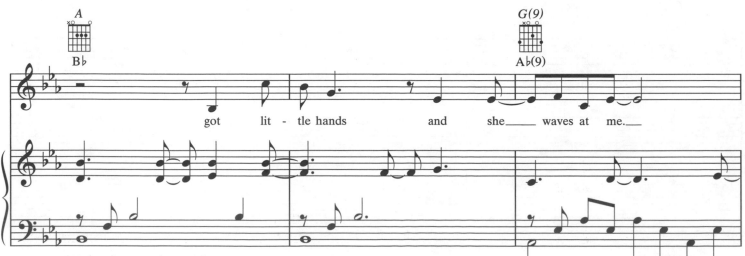

27

Chorus:

Hello World - 12 - 3
34914

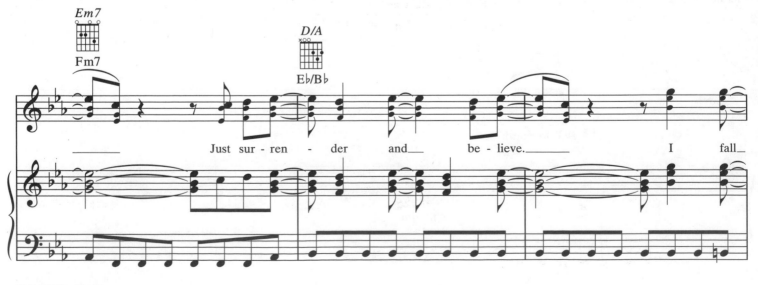

down on___ my knees.___ Well, hel - lo, world,_____

hel - lo, world,_____ hel - lo, world._

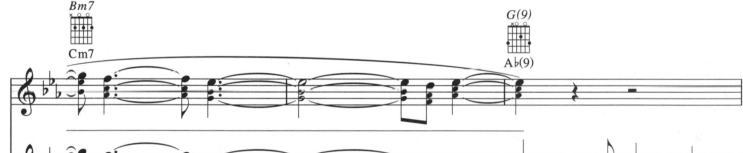

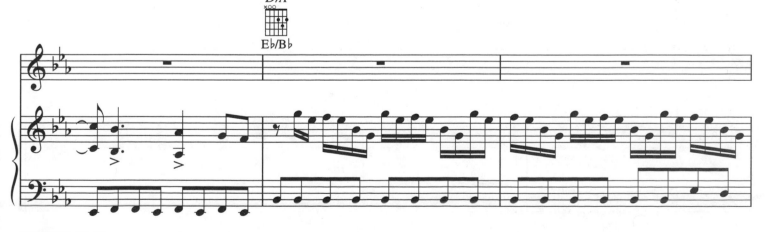

PERFECT DAY

Words and Music by
DAVE HAYWOOD, CHARLES KELLEY,
HILLARY SCOTT and JERRY FLOWERS

Moderate country beat ♩ = 100

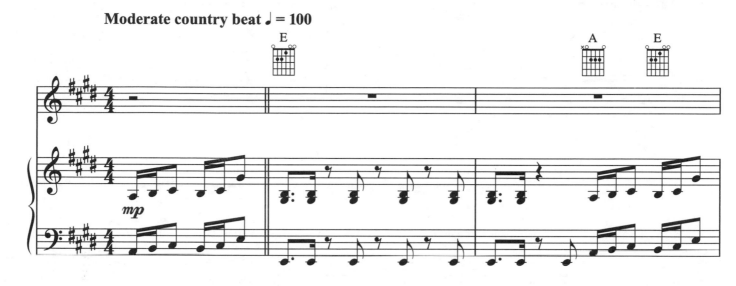

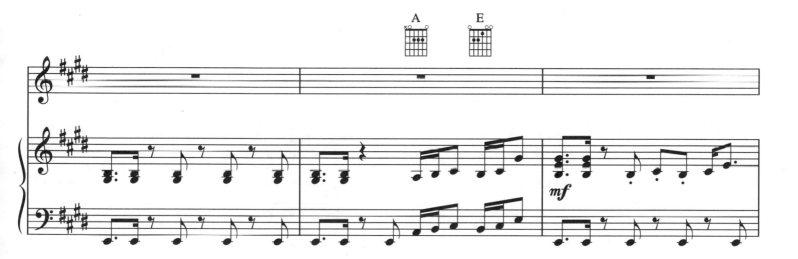

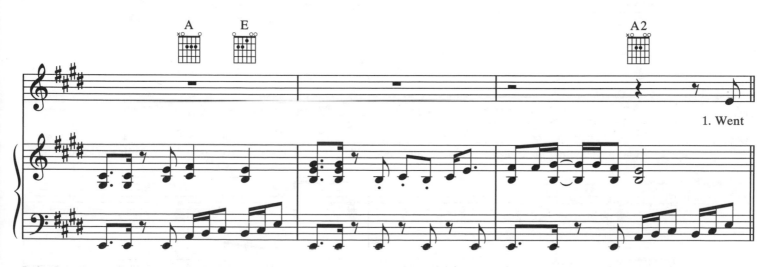

1. Went

Perfect Day - 7 - 1
34914

Verse 1:

2. Met up__

Verses 2 & 3:

E

Verse 2 (sing for Verse 2 only):

__ with some friends out - side of town,__ they were head-ed towards__ the lake.__ I hopped

A

Verse 3 (sing for Verse 3 only):

moon came out and the fire__ burned, ev - 'ry - bod - y was sing-ing a - long__ to some

Chorus:

C#m7 ... A2

day. What I'd give if I____ could find____ a way to

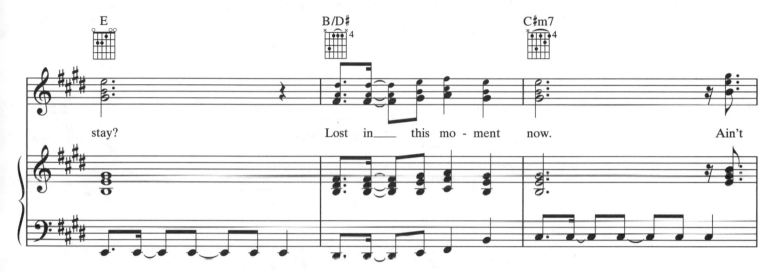

E ... B/D# ... C#m7

stay? Lost in____ this mo - ment now. Ain't

A2 ... D ... *To Coda*

wor - ried 'bout____ to - mor - row when you're bus - y liv - ing

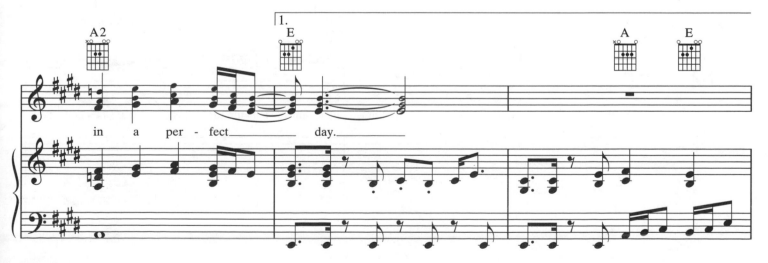

A2 ... E ... A ... E

in a per - fect_____ day._____

Perfect Day - 7 - 7
34914

LOVE THIS PAIN

Words and Music by
MARV GREEN and JASON SELLERS

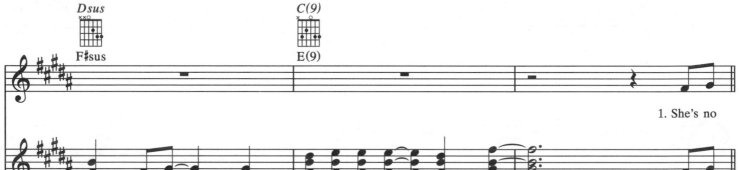

1. She's no

good for me.__ I know that she's__ a wild - flow - er.

on a - gain__ and off a - gain__ sit - u - a - tion.

love my heart all bust-ed up. Some-thing 'bout her, we

just don't work, but I can't walk____ a - way.____ It's like I

love this pain.____

2. It's just an ____ It's like I

It's like I love this pain.

It's like I love this___ pain._____

(Why can't I walk a - way?)

WHEN YOU GOT A GOOD THING

Words and Music by
DAVE HAYWOOD, CHARLES KELLEY,
HILLARY SCOTT and RIVERS RUTHERFORD

Oh, there's gon - na be__ some up__ and downs,_ but with you__

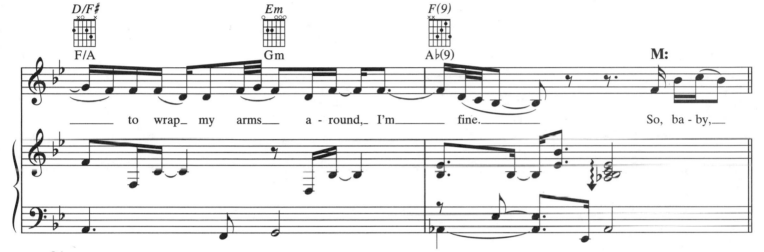

___ to wrap_ my arms__ a - round,_ I'm_____ fine. So, ba - by,__

M:

𝄋 *Chorus:*

Both: hold on tight. Don't let go.

Hold on to the love we're_ mak - ing, 'cause, ba - by, when the

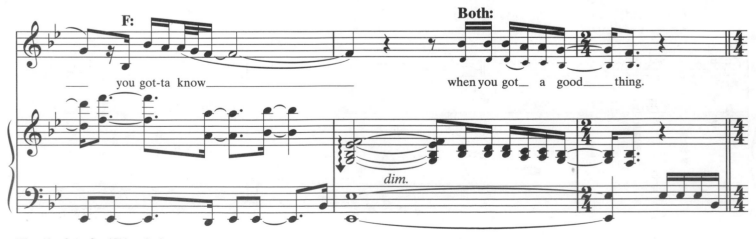

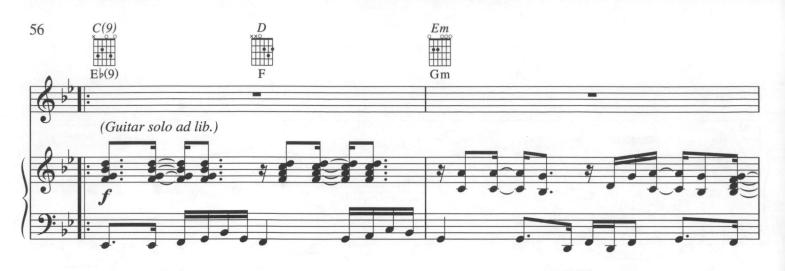

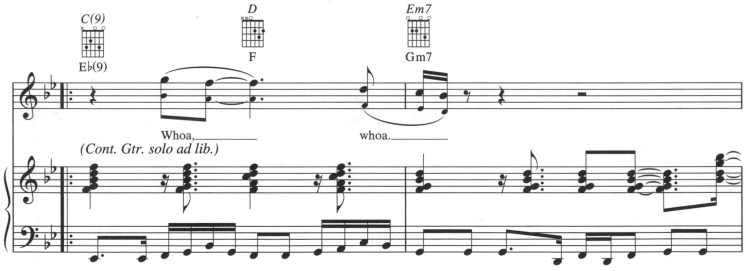

Repeat ad lib. and fade

STARS TONIGHT

Words and Music by
DAVE HAYWOOD, CHARLES KELLEY,
HILLARY SCOTT and MONTY POWELL

Moderate rock beat ♩ = 120

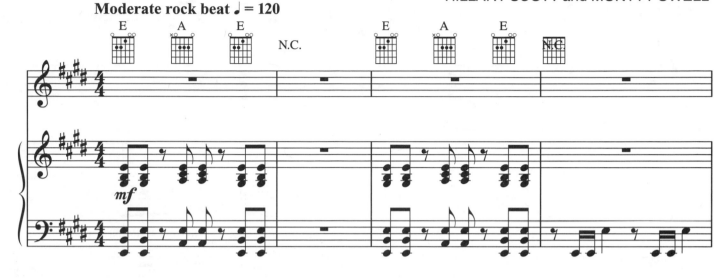

Male:

1. Girls_

Verse 1:

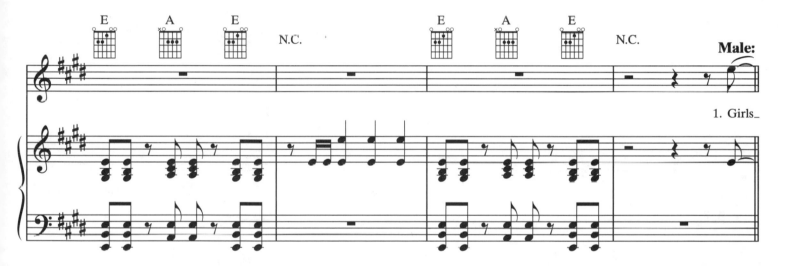

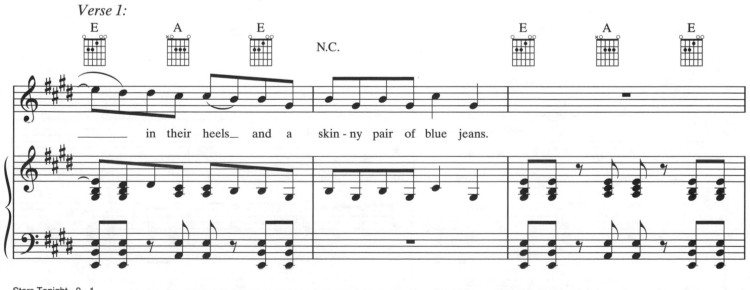

_____ in their heels_ and a skin-ny pair of blue jeans.

Stars Tonight - 9 - 1
34914

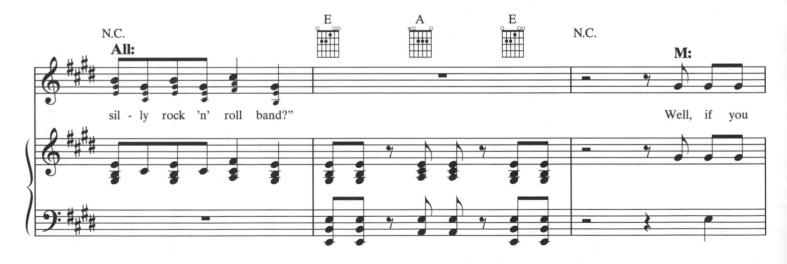

It's the lights,_____ it's the high,_____ it's the roar_

_ of a crowd_ on a Fri - day night. **Both:** And ev - 'ry - bod - y's scream - in' out

%% *Chorus:*

"Yeah,_____ yeah,_____ yeah."_ And

ev - 'ry - bod - y's sing - in' now, "Yeah,_____ yeah,_____ yeah."

Get on your feet if it feels___ good,___ it feels___

right,___ 'cause we're all stars___ to - night.___ So, sing it out:

"Yeah, yeah,_____ yeah."___

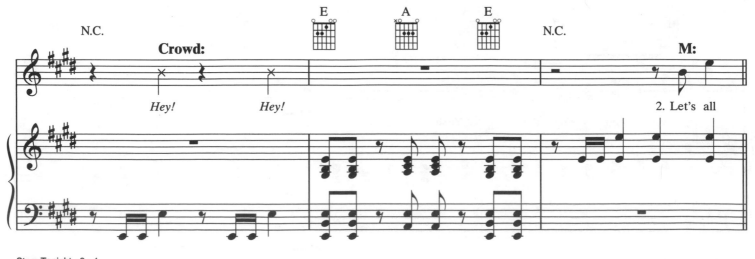

Crowd:

Hey! *Hey!*

M:

2. Let's all

Verse 2:

get a lit - tle row - dy; gon - na par - ty all night long.____

And, boys, sway____ with your girls____ when we play a lit - tle slow____ song.____

Put your hands____ in the air;____ shine a

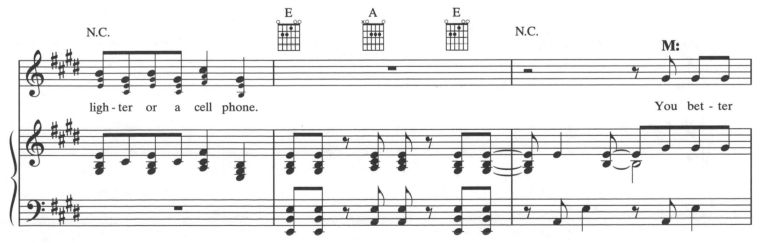

ligh - ter or a cell phone. You bet - ter

buy an-oth-er round;__ we ain't__ go-in' home,__ no.

On the floor,_____ in the stands,_____ to-night

D.S. ℅ al Coda

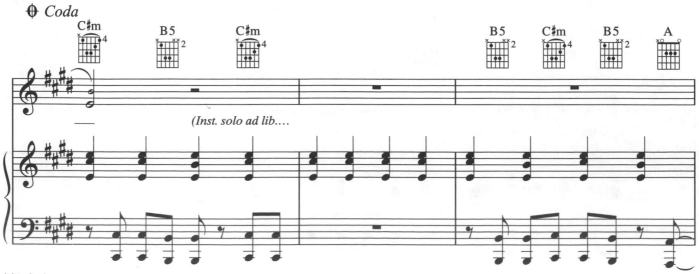

we're all in_____ the band._____ And we're scream-in' out,

Coda

(Inst. solo ad lib....

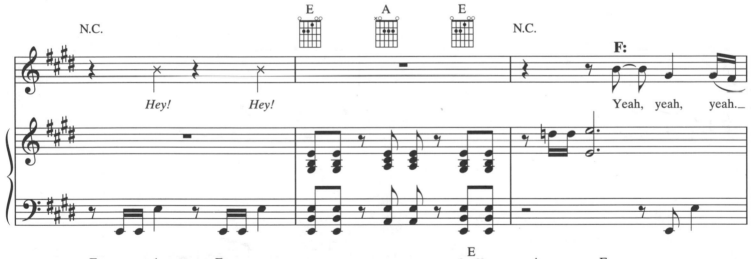

Stars Tonight - 9 - 9
34914

IF I KNEW THEN

Words and Music by
CHARLES KELLEY, MONTY POWELL
and ANNA WILSON

first time that I saw you look-ing like you did we were young,

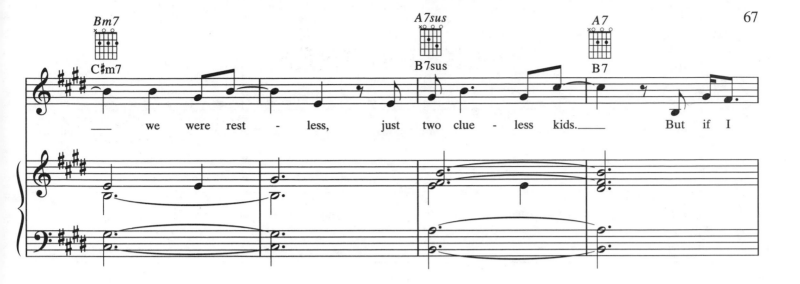

we were rest - less, just two clue - less kids.___ But if I

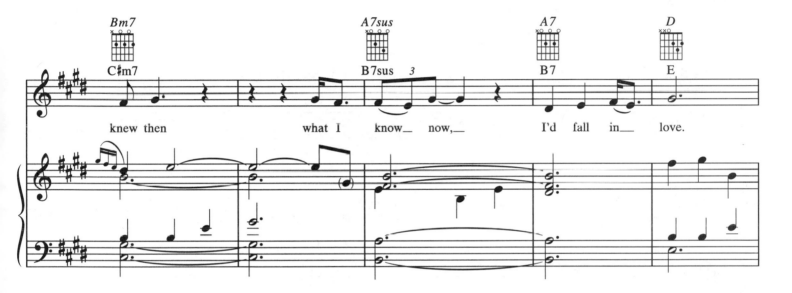

knew then   what I   know___ now,___   I'd fall in___ love.

Verse 2 (sing for Verse 2 only):

Both: 2. On a bus___   in   Chi - ca   -   go

Verse 3 (sing for Verse 3 only):

mer night   in   Au - gust   in the

mp - mf

Chorus:

love on - ly comes___ once in a while,___ knocks on your door___ and throws you a smile,___ and takes ev - 'ry breath,___ leaves ev - 'ry scar,___ speaks to your soul___ and sings to your heart.___ And if I

SOMETHING 'BOUT A WOMAN

Words and Music by
DAVE HAYWOOD, CHARLES KELLEY,
HILLARY SCOTT and CRAIG WISEMAN

like some___ kind of Heav - en that's pour - in'___ down___ on___ me.___

She's a child,___ she's a la -

dy,___ she's got ev - 'ry - thing that

I could ev - er need.___

78

Yeah, there's some-thing 'bout a wom-an in - deed.

To Coda ⊕

(Slide Guitar)

She

READY TO LOVE AGAIN

Words and Music by
DAVE HAYWOOD, CHARLES KELLEY,
HILLARY SCOTT and MIKE BUSBEE

Moderately ♩ = 108

1. Seems I was walk-ing in the wrong di - rec - tion.

I bare-ly rec-og-nized my own re-flec - tion, oh.___ Scared of

About the Band

Need You Now is the title of Lady Antebellum's second album, lifted from its leadoff track, which explores the desperate longings that make separated lovers yearn to reconnect in the wee small hours of the morning. But that "need you now" mantra isn't just a refrain that exes leave on each other's answering machines in the middle of the night. That message could just as easily serve as an SOS sent out to the group from fans and the music industry. The band's first album, from 2007, was the very rare freshman effort to debut at No. 1 and/or go Platinum these days, and the emotional connection that was forged with audiences over the short course of several hit singles and high-profile tours clearly left 'em wanting—no, *needing*—more.

Thankfully, unlike in the song, we won't even have to do any drunk-dialing to get what we've craved. Less than two years after the trio's debut first hit stores with a splash, *Need You Now* is at hand to satisfy the hunger. There's been no lull in the roll Lady Antebellum is on. They've had back-to-back chart-topping singles, proceeding directly from the previous effort's "I Run to You" hitting the top spot in July to their "Need You Now" single enjoying a five-week run at No. 1 just prior to the new album's release. Since then it has also become a major hit at pop radio as well, and was frequently at the top of the all-genre iTunes single chart.

Selling more than a million copies in the first month, *Need You Now* comes right on the heels of a prominent Grammy award for Best Performance by a Country Group for "I Run To You" in January and two key wins at November's CMA Awards - Single of the Year ("I Run to You") and Vocal Group of the Year.

The CMAs recognition *did* bring about a fairly urgent sense of ante-upping. "It puts expectations on us," says Charles Kelley, who shares lead vocal duties with Hillary Scott. "We already felt like there was a lot to prove after winning Best New Artist the year before—like people are invested in us and saying 'All right, go get 'em.' Which is why we're excited to get this album out."

"I'll be honest," says Hillary. "Somebody asked me if I was on such a high about the awards, and I said, 'Absolutely.' But I was thinking to myself, 'I'm also a little terrified.' Because you hit a point like that and you really can't go backwards…"

"Well, we *can* go backwards," chimes in Charles, the pragmatist, laughing nervously.

"If anything, though, it makes us want to work harder and record even better songs and continue to grow as performers and prove that we're deserving of it," says Hillary.

You can hear that burning flame throughout *Need You Now*, which continues their delicate—or delicately rowdy—balance of emotional, gut-level balladry and high-octane, arena-ready rockers. Members of the trio co-wrote eight of the 11 tracks and were able to rely on a much tighter intra-band bond than they had when they were crafting the first album, which was recorded not that long after old pals Charles and Dave got together with new acquaintance Hillary to form the group back in 2006.

"Because of the success of the first record, we could get with some really great songwriters that'll take an appointment with us now," says Dave, the group's guitarist and background vocalist. "But more importantly, the three of us are the closest we've ever been as friends. Out on the road, we've spent almost every single day together for the past three and a half years. So by the time we were writing songs for this record, I think we'd all learned how to interact with each other better. We can write songs individually, but we definitely have something special when we do it together, and that's gotten elevated. I know what Hillary is thinking, I know what Charles is thinking, and I think we play off each other a lot better."

"We would know if something personally was going on with Hillary," says Charles. "We would say, 'How about we tap into your personal hell for a little bit? Let's bring that out in a song!' When we're all songwriting, we know what's going on in everybody's lives."

"When they let me talk about it!" laughs Hillary, suggesting that there might be a slight gender divide in the group when it comes to complete candor. "I could see their eyes glaze over. But when we all get into talking about these things together, you get a song like 'Ready to Love Again' (the album's closer) out of it."

"Songwriting," Charles asserts, "is almost kind of like our little group therapy."

Any such therapeutic discussions don't involve too many regrets about professional roads not taken. Least of all would they have any reason to regret having abandoned the option of solo careers to come together as a group, at a time when the conventional wisdom was that individuals usually work better than bands in marketing country music. There were a few tentative moments during Lady Antebellum's formation, though, as Charles and Dave danced around the idea of doing anything so brash as forming a *band*.

"When we met Hillary," says Charles, "she had all these contacts in town and had some development deals—just basically really tied into the system." She had a bit of a head start on understanding the business, too, being the daughter of the well-known singer Linda Davis. "We were like, 'All right, she's got one of the best voices. We've got to write for her project.' So we got together with her and wrote 'All We'd Ever Need' and 'Love Don't Live Here Anymore,' which ended up on the first record. We thought, 'Wow, this is really great,' but we didn't want her to think we were little weasels trying to get in there and ride her coattails."

Hillary: "And I was sitting there thinking, 'This takes so much of the pressure off!' You could not pay me enough money to go back and NOT be in a band. Being a solo artist wasn't for me. I wasn't cut out for it. I didn't handle the pressure at all." Even now, she eagerly confesses, "I'm the baby of the group. But I've grown up!"

For the band itself, there was an element of growing up in public, a little. The debut album itself was an immediate smash, debuting at No. 1 on the country albums chart, an example of a rare phenomenon that is referred to in the arcane parlance of the music industry as… love at first sight. But their first real tour was an arena tour, opening for Martina McBride, and they acknowledge that, as a still fairly newly founded combo, there were rough patches in their performances. "It felt a little early, even though the crowds were really gracious and great to us," remembers Charles. "Then we said, 'All right, this is what we need to improve on,' and we went out to these fairs and festivals and made plenty of mistakes in a safer environment where it wasn't quite as big a deal if you were to mess up. We did close to 200 shows our first year. Lost a ton of money, because we were doing smaller shows that cost us twice as much as we were getting paid."

Their live performance chops finally properly in order, they planned to halt their rigorous touring schedule to concentrate on the second album, which they'd planned to put out in 2009. They wrapped up a tour supporting Kenny Chesney and had recorded much of the sophomore effort when the call came in to support Keith Urban on his tour. And faster than you can say "Who Wouldn't Wanna Be Me?," they took the offer, even while regretting delaying the new album. In hindsight, the postponement no longer felt like a mixed blessing, but a complete one.

"At the time we were bummed out, because we had just cut the first half of the record, and we had a big batch of songs and we were ready to go back in and finish," explains Charles. "But because we didn't, we had time to write three or four better songs, and then we found a couple of outside songs that we didn't write that we just had to do"—namely, "American Honey" and "Hello World." "It was the best thing that ever happened to us, having that gap of time before we came back in and finished the back half of the record. It totally in my mind took the record from here to here," he says, placing his hand a few inches even higher than his 6-foot-6 frame.

This time, the band nabbed co-producer credit for themselves, with Dave acknowledged by all as the member most comfortable with the ways of the studio. Continuing on in the director's chair from the last album is veteran Paul Worley, who produced smash albums by some of mainstream country's biggest stars. "Paul trusts our gut instincts of where we think things should go, but there's no substitute for his 30 years of experience," Charles says. "There's not anything he hasn't tried on a record in the past, so he's able to know why this wouldn't work or this would. I was always the one to want him to stack guitars and thicken the damn thing up, and he was always like, 'Man, let this thing lie back and live more organic and let every instrument shine through.' Without someone like that keeping you down, you'd go in there and botch up what was beautiful about the thing in the first place. If I'd just known when I was listening to those first couple of Dixie Chicks records that I would be working with this guy and he would be a fan of what we're doing, it would have been too wild to believe."

Of course, Worley realizes that there's no need to "stack" anything that would get in the way of those harmonies, or the group's traded-off lead vocals.

With male and female front-people, Hillary says, "I think we're able to say so much more and reach so many more people. Because there's no way that I could have been able to put my vocal on a song like 'Hello World' and make it believable like Charles did." The diffused focus also makes for a more dynamic live experience. "When it's a song I'm singing lead on, Charles and Dave can go be buddy-buddy on stage. When Charles and I do a duet, we can, without being too theatrical, almost play out the songs and tell the story a little bit more, whether we're making it dramatic or fun and flirty."

Charles agrees: "Having the two lead vocals there can take people into different journeys. And I think there are people who are just naturally gonna gravitate to her voice that aren't gonna gravitate to mine, and vice versa. And then on top of it, you've got this harmony potential, with Dave. When we mix the record, we don't even realize how important the three-part harmony is until it's not there. In the mix, they sometimes tend to blend in together, these two men's voices. But it warms it up so much. If there was one little piece of the puzzle that

wasn't there on anything, or if his voice was too high or vice versa... We definitely feel very fortunate that we found each other and it all happened."

Not every song on *Need You Now* is a heavy one. A tune like "Stars Tonight" is intended as a "get up on your feet live song," as Dave laughingly puts it, "there to remind our fans, 'Hey, we're the ones that sing 'Lookin' for a Good Time,' too!'" But for every dose of sheer escapism on the album, there are two shots of unvarnished truth.

"I was up until 5 in the morning one night while we were making the album, writing Dave and Charles an email," says Hillary. "I stepped back from it and just looked at why we wrote or chose each song, and it hit me that all of these songs are just about feeling to the utmost of your ability. Whether it's 'I'm so desperate for you, I miss you so much, I need you *NOW*' desperation,' or 'American Honey,' which is nostalgic and wanting to go back to that innocence and sweetness. And then you have 'Hello World,' which is this man's story of this awakening in his soul, opening his eyes and seeing what's important in his life again."

"When you're in the valleys, they suck and it's not fun, but you appreciate the mountaintop way more whenever you've gone through something tough," Hillary continues. "That's how I personally try to live my life, just enjoying every moment— but when it hurts, *let* it hurt. Because you loved something or someone so much, it's only natural to grieve that. So that's what I verbalized to them, that I was proud of our ability to be that honest and just lay it all out there."

Need You Now has a good deal of subtle mirroring in its themes. "American Honey," a gorgeous ballad about being awakened to life by wistful remembrance of things past, is followed by "Hello World," which deals with the same kind of wake-up call, but looking toward a more hopeful future. The album is bookended with two of its most emotionally naked numbers; the closing "Ready to Love Again," which Hillary calls "probably the most personal song on the record," provides a sort of answer to the title track, which opens the album.

They're still a little surprised that "Need You Now," as a single, made such a quick trip to the top of the chart. "Honestly, I thought it would be a grind," Charles says. "But I know there's something honest in it that people gravitate toward."

To paraphrase *Casablanca*, this feels like the second step in a beautiful friendship. "With 'I Run to You' being our first No. 1, it was really the first moment where I felt like with us as artists and the audience, the puzzle pieces fit," Hillary says. "They figured out more about what we wanted to say and the kind of artists we were, and that's what they ended up liking. And then the same thing with having our second No. 1 be 'Need You Now,' this song that we believe in its honesty and vulnerability so much. It's exciting to feel like that bond is just growing, and we're getting tighter in that relationship. Like, they get us! We get them! This is great!" Here's to many more years of both sides getting their needs met.